ONCE UPON A TIME DINOSAURS USED TO LIVE

All rights are reserved. No part of this book may be reproduced or transmitted in any form or by any means including photocopying or recording.

Copyright © 2022 Moumita Majumdar
M.A. in English Literature

ONCE UPON A TIME DINOSAURS USED TO LIVE

People have only been on Earth for about 2.5 million years. Dinosaurs lived on Earth for about 160 million years. The word "dinosaur" was coined by British paleontologist Richard Owen in 1842. It is a Greek word meaning "terrible lizard."

Nobody knows precisely what was the lifespan of a dinosaur. Some scientists believe that some dinosaurs have lived for 200 years. Scientists assume that there are many dinosaurs still undiscovered and that there could be as many as 1,850 species

Explorer Roy Chapman Andrews discovered the first dinosaur nest known to science in 1923 in the Gobi Mountains of Mongolia.

The first dinosaurs were carnivores or meat-eaters. Later herbivores and omnivores appeared. Most dinosaurs were vegetarians.

Dinosaurs were often used to swallow large rocks. These rocks remained in the stomach and helped them to digest their food.

Most meat-eating dinosaurs had bones filled with air. Although their bones were huge, they weren't as heavy as they looked.

All dinosaurs used to lay eggs. About 40 kinds of dinosaur eggs have been discovered.

Allosaurus

Allosaurus were carnivores. The meaning of their name is 'different lizard'. They used to found in the Late Jurassic Period. Their length was about 28 feet. They had three fingers on their "arms" for tearing meat. They weighed about 4 tons.

Ankylosaurus

The Ankylosaurus was a big dinosaur that had huge plates of body armor to protect itself from attackers, and if that wasn't enough it also had a massive tail club that was strong enough to break very hard bones. Ankylosaurus lived around 66 million years ago. Their length was around 9 meters and a weight of around 6000 kg. They were herbivores mean plant eaters and had small teeth relative to their body size.

Apatosaurus

Apatosaurus, also called Brontosaurus, was a true giant dinosaur that lived about 150 million years ago. The Apatosaurus is one of the most large animals ever on earth. It was 75 feet long and 50,000 pounds. It had a very long neck and tail and a small head. The Apatosaurus walked on four legs. It was very slow-moving creature due to its large weight.

They had a small head and brain. The Apatosaurus was an herbivore, meaning it only ate plants. He had to eat a lot of plants every day for their large size. He did not chew his food, but instead had stones called gastroliths in his stomach which helped to digest their food.

Archaeopteryx

Archaeopteryx was a pigeon-size creature. They lived in the Late Jurassic Period around 150 million years ago. The length of an Archaeopteryx was up to 1.8 feet. They used to weight up to 2.2 pounds. They were carnivore and most likely used to eat smaller reptiles, mammals, insects, an fish.

Brachiosaurus

These dinosaurs were herbivores, meaning were plant eaters. They lived in the Late Jurassic Period. Their length was around 26 meters and They weighed about 40 tons . They lived about 154 to 153 million years ago - in the late Jurassic period. They had longer legs at the front than at the back. They could reach up 9 meters high.

Carnotaurus

This dinosaur was a meat eater, it weighed around 2000 kg. They had unique eyes that turned forward, rather than on the side like most other dinosaurs. Carnotaurus lived around 66 million years ago. They lived in an area of South America known as Patagonia. They were discovered in 1985 by a famous Argentine paleontologist named Jose Bonaparte.

They were about 8 feet long and weighed between 1500 and 2500 kg. They had very small arms and fingers that did not move.

Dakosaurus

Dakosaurus was a prehistoric crocodile, except it lived in the sea and had no scaly skin. They use to found in Late Jurassic Period through the Early Cretaceous Period in North and South America.

They were a little smaller than a saltwater crocodile and weighed more than a cow. They were a Carnivore and lived about 150 to 130 million years ago. They used to eat fish, shellfish and possibly even squids and other smaller marine reptiles that existed in the oceans at that time.

Dilophosaurus

The dilophosaurus lived 193 million years ago, during the early Jurassic Period. They had a large crest on its skull, made from delicate bone. They used to be 23 feet long. They had hollow bones and a long neck, legs, and tail. Dilophosaurus probably used its claws and arms for hunting and fighting.

Dimorphodon

They used to found in Middle-late Jurassic Period. It was discovered in early 19th century in England by fossil-hunter Mary Anning. They had Large head and long tail. They used to have two different types of teeth in their jaws. longer ones in front and shorter, flatter ones in back. Dimorphodon is one of those animals that looks like it was assembled wrong out of the box.

Elasmosaurus

They existed around 93.9 million years ago. Elasmosaurus a type of marine reptile. The first Elasmosaurus fossil was discovered in 1868. They used to live in a marine environment. They were carnivorous. They used to have enormous size, reaching up to 46 feet long. It was discovered by Edward Cope, he mistakenly believed that the creature's neck was in fact an extremely long tail. They used to give live birth instead of laying eggs.

Metriorhynchus

Metriorhynchus was a prehistoric crocodile that lived about 155 million years ago in the Late Jurassic period. The fossils of this crocodile were first discovered in the 19th century in England, in France in Germany.One of the most interesting facts about them is that they can be found in about 12 different species. This crocodile was about 10 feet long, weighed 500 pounds, and had skin very different from modern era crocodiles or alligators. They used to have smooth skin.

Parasaurolophus

Parasaurolophus lived around 76.5 million years ago, during the late Cretaceous period. Parasaurolophus's most distinctive feature was a large crest on its head. With that crest they used to make make loud trumpeting calls. They were in between 9.5 and 10 m in length. They were able could walk on either two or four legs.
Their tail was thin, but unusually tall.

Parasaurus

They were herbivores. They had large head crests they used for trumpeting that they used to talk to each other. Their length was up to 33 feet. They were herbivores (plant eaters) that used their strong back legs to reach higher branches.

Plesiosaurus

The plesiosaurs were large, carnivorous marine reptiles. plesiosaurus lived around 245 million years ago. Mary Anning was the first to discover a fossils of a complete plesiosaur. The fossil was missing its skull, but in 1823 she found another one, this time complete with its skull. Plesiosaurs had many bones in their flippers, making them flexible. They were mainly piscivorous (fish-eaters).

Pliosaurs

Pliosaurs were big and vicious looking predators.The pliosaurs were a group of large submarine predators with short necks and large heads. Their sizes ranged from 2 to 15 metres, They lived in the Mesozoic seas, and likely hunted almost anything that swam. Pliosaurs had very large fins instead of legs and had massive heads with rows of sharp teeth. Pliosaurs' is related to the modern fresh water crocodile.

Pteranodon

The Pteranodon lived during the Late Cretaceous Period. The most recognizable feature of the Pteranodon was their large cranial crests. Pteranodons had no teeth, but rather a sharp beak like some modern day birds. Male Pteranodons were considerably larger than female Pteranodons.The average wingspan of a male Pteranodon is 18 feet. They used to be in between 44 pounds to 205 pounds.

Raptorex

Raptorex used to live around 243 million years ago. it was known to inhabit regions of China, Mongolia, and Central Asia. The specimen of fossils is now housed and preserved as evidence of its discovery. Raptorex evolved from Tyrannosaurs. While many herbivore dinosaurs were found to live in a group, meat-eaters often led a solitary life or hunted in packs The body length of the Raptorex ranged from 8.2 ft and was tallest at its hips. It was about 10 ft tall.

Rhamphorhynchus

Rhamphorhynchus fossils suggest that they were flying reptiles that existed during the dinosaur age. They existed during the late Jurrasic period in the regions of Europe and Africa. The fossil prints of these creatures were mainly found in Spain, England, Portugal, and Tanzania.

Spinosaurus

Spinosaurus were the biggest carnivorous dinosaur. The meaning of Spinosaurus is 'Spine Lizard'. They lived in the Cretaceous Period. Their length was up to 59 feet. They weighed up to 20 tons. One intersting fact about them was The Spinosaurus had powerful jaws with straight teeth. Most other meat eating dinosaurs had curved teeth.

Stegosaurus

Stegosaurs lived about 150 million years ago in the Late Jurassic Period. The first fossil was discovered by Professor Othniel Marsh in 1877. Stegosaurus had brains the size of ping pong balls. Their length was up to 30 feet. They weighed 2 tons. The Stegosaurus was a plant eater, which we call a herbivore. It is believed to have eaten plants such as mosses, ferns, horsetails, cycads, and conifers or fruits. The Stegosaurus dinosaur lived in what is now called western North America.

Triceratops

Triceratops lived in the Late Cretaceous Period. Triceratops lived in the marshes and forests of North America. Triceratops fossils have been found in Colorado, Wyoming, and Montana. Triceratops was squat and powerfully built, roughly the size of an elephant. It walked on four, thick legs, and had a short but powerful tail. It could reach up to 30 feet in length and 10 feet in height. It could weigh up to 24,250 pounds. Triceratops' skull was one of the largest in proportion to body size among all land animals.

Tyrannosaurus rex

Tyrannosaurus rex is possibly the most well-known dinosaur due to its huge size. The skull of a Tyrannosaurus rex alone measured up to 1.5m long. Tyrannosaurus rex measured up to 13m in length, 4m at the hip, and could weigh up to 7 tons. They were one of the biggest meat eaters. Their arms were too short to reach its mouth. They used to live in forests, near rivers, and in areas that were open and full of prey.

Velociraptors

Velociraptor fossils have been found in the Gobi Desert, which covers southern Mongolia and parts of northern China. Velociraptor had a sharp, deadly, sickle-shaped, retractable, 3.5-inch claw on each foot. They were able to run up to 60 km/hr. They used to hunt in packs. They used to eat reptiles, amphibians, insects, small dinosaurs, and mammals. Velociraptor was roughly the size of a small turkey. Adult Velociraptors grew up to 6.8 feet long.

www.ingramcontent.com/pod-product-compliance
Lightning Source LLC
LaVergne TN
LVHW021319160826
845679LV00001B/415
* 9 7 9 8 3 5 1 9 1 8 9 1 4 *